THE EXTREME

HORROR STICKER BOOK

500+ Stickers
to Keep You Up at Night

Illustrated by Andy Price

Adams Media

New York London Toronto Sydney New Delhi

Adams Media
An Imprint of Simon & Schuster, LLC
100 Technology Center Drive
Stoughton, Massachusetts 02072

First Adams Media trade paperback edition August 2024

ADAMS MEDIA and colophon are registered trademarks of Simon & Schuster, LLC.

Simon & Schuster: Celebrating 100 Years of Publishing in 2024

For information about special discounts for bulk purchases, please contact Simon & Schuster Special Sales at 1-866-506-1949 or business@simonandschuster.com.

The Simon & Schuster Speakers Bureau can bring authors to your live event. For more information or to book an event, contact the Simon & Schuster Speakers Bureau at 1-866-248-3049 or visit our website at www.simonspeakers.com.

Interior design by Erin Alexander
Illustrations by Andy Price

Manufactured in China

10 9 8 7 6 5 4 3 2 1

ISBN 978-1-5072-2252-2

INTRODUCTION

Screaming skulls with watchful eyes.

Ferocious chain saws dripping blood.

Groaning monsters poised to attack.

These horrors loom ever closer—they appear in your notebook, on your water bottle, and even on your phone case—with this terrifyingly addictive collection of stickers that go bump in the night!

This devilishly diverting sticker collection has tons of perfect scares to add to your favorite stuff, with peel-and-stick illustrations of slashers, haunted dolls, restless graves, and frightening catchphrases like "Don't Scream." With more than five hundred stickers featuring horrors of all kinds, you'll be able to cover every surface with scary art—and make your world a little darker and more twisted!

FINAL Girl

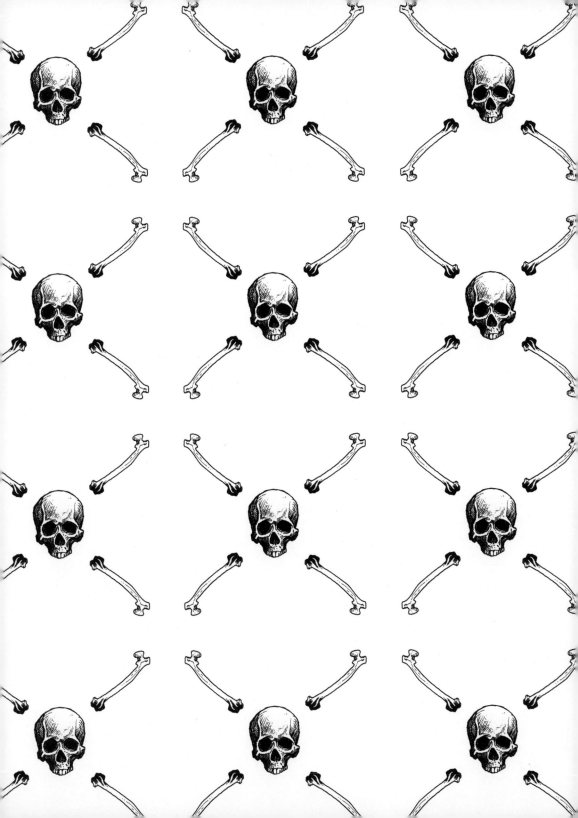

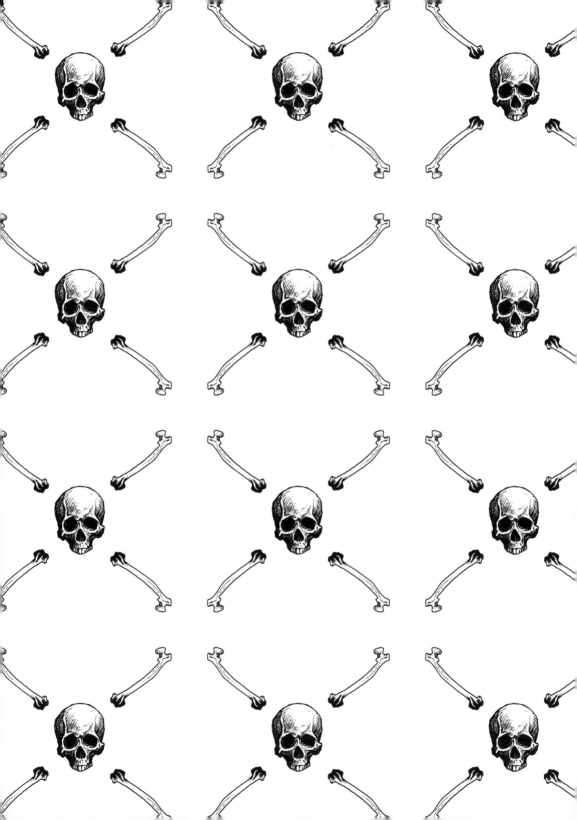

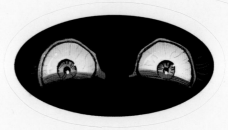

DON'T YOU JUST LOVE IT WHEN THEY

SCREAM

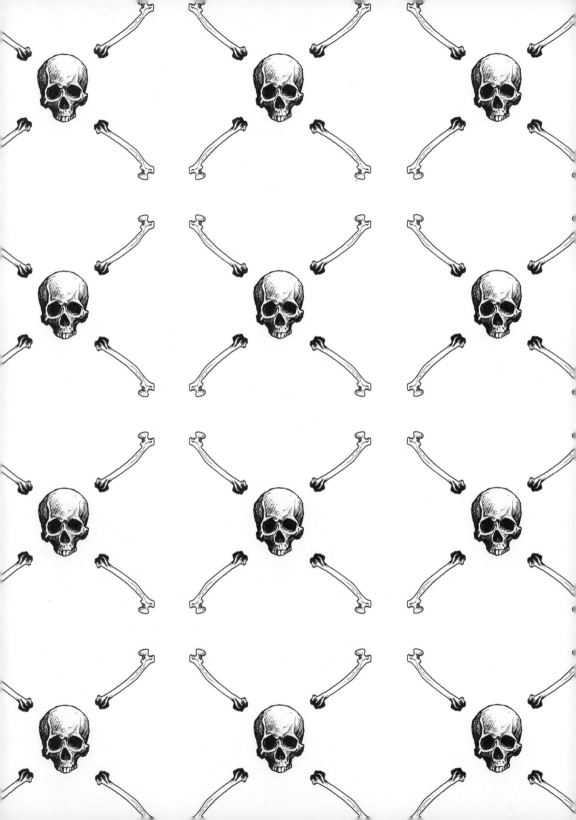

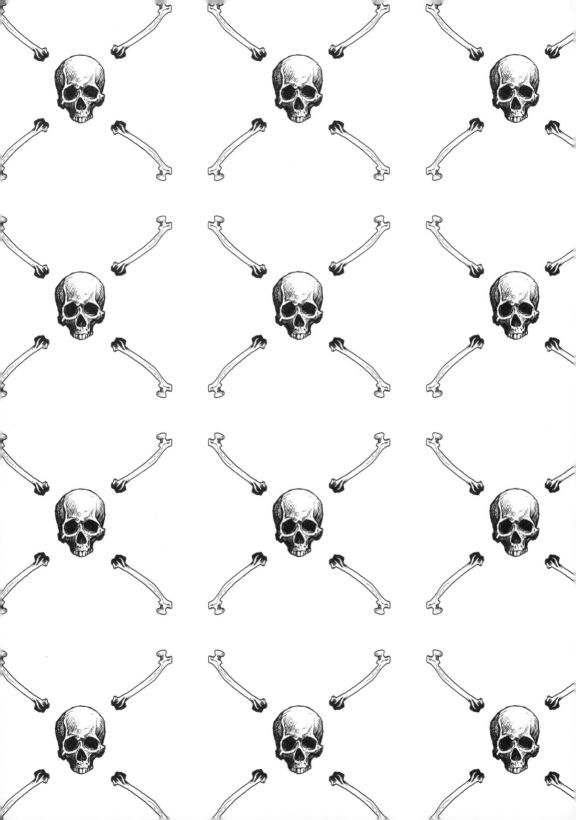

HEY, GOOD LOOKIN'! WE'LL BE BACK TO PICK YOU UP...

LATER

FINAL BOY

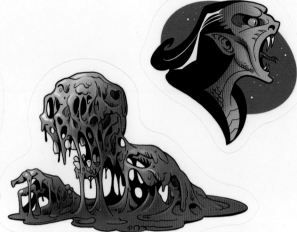

GOOD MOURNING

STAY CREEPY

LAUGH 'TIL YOU DIE

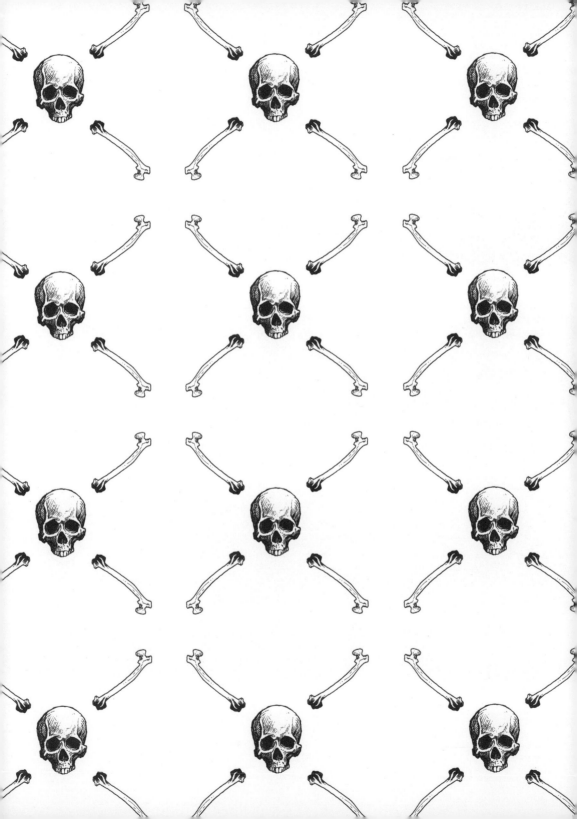

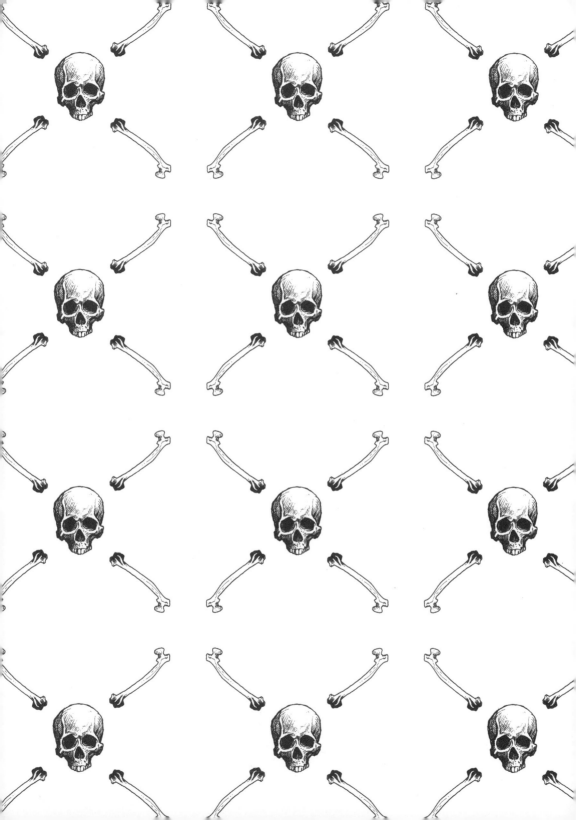

CREATURE OF THE NIGHT

POISON

BE AFRAID

HORROR

Die Screaming

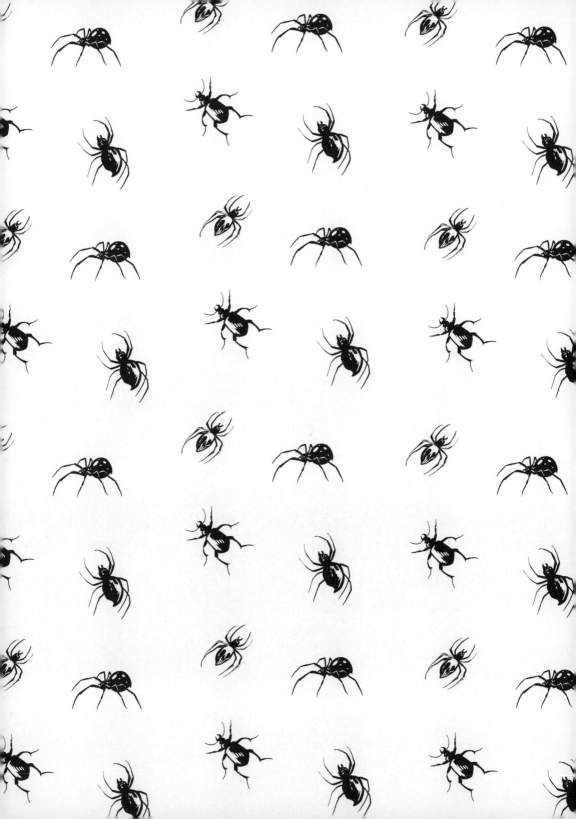

DEAD
MAN'S
HAND

NEVER
SAY
NEVER

RIP

RIP

A G-G-GHOST!

R I P

Ferryman's
FUNERAL HOME
"THERE AIN'T NO USE TO DENY IT...
SOMEDAY, YOU'RE GONNA BUY IT!"
GROUP RATES • FREE PARKING

GRAVEYARD
FAN CLUB
DIG IT!

Stayin'
Alive

STILL
DEAD

OUT TO
LUNCH
BACK IN 5

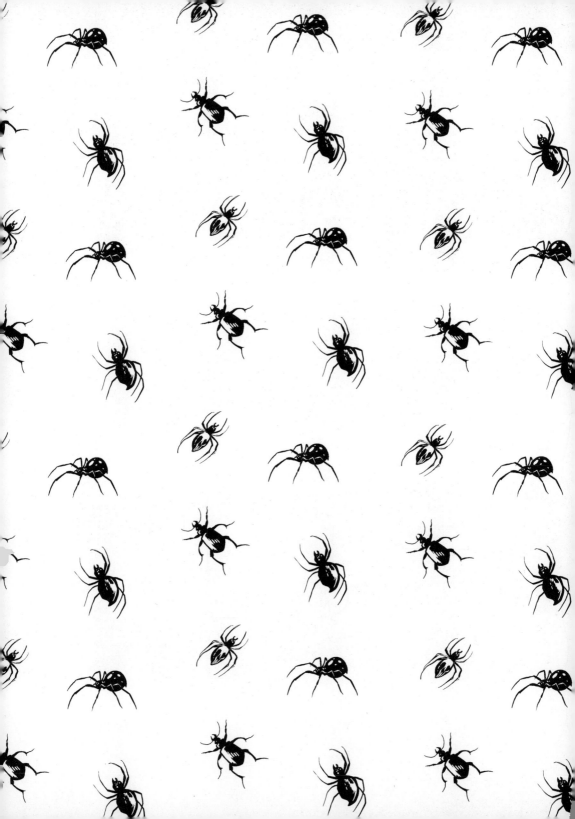

I SCREAM MAN

CREEP

MONSTER

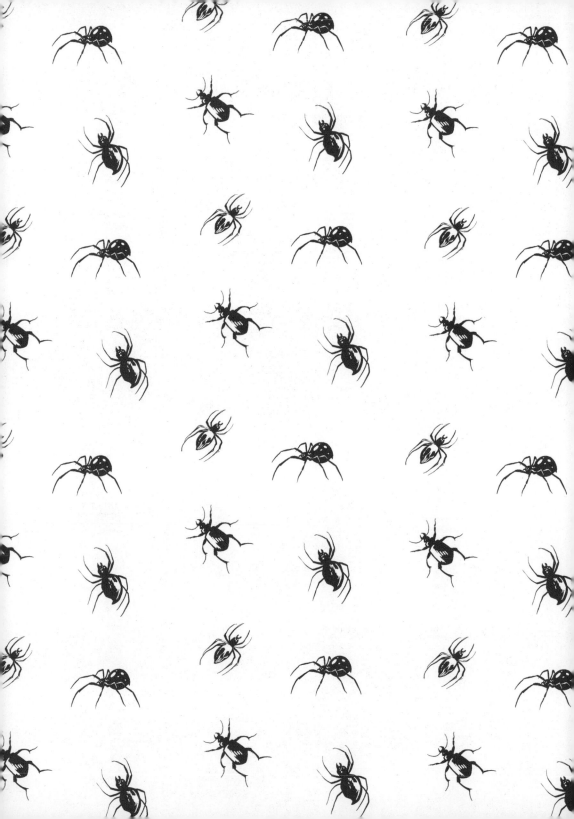

Drive Like
Hell
You'll Get There!

Grammy

ATTACH TO TOE	NAME OF DECEASED			CASE NO. _____	
	AGE	SEX	RACE	WEIGHT	HEIGHT
	PLACE OF DEATH			DATE OF DEATH	
	CAUSE OF DEATH				
	PHYSICIAN				
	FUNERAL DIRECTOR				
	COMMENTS				

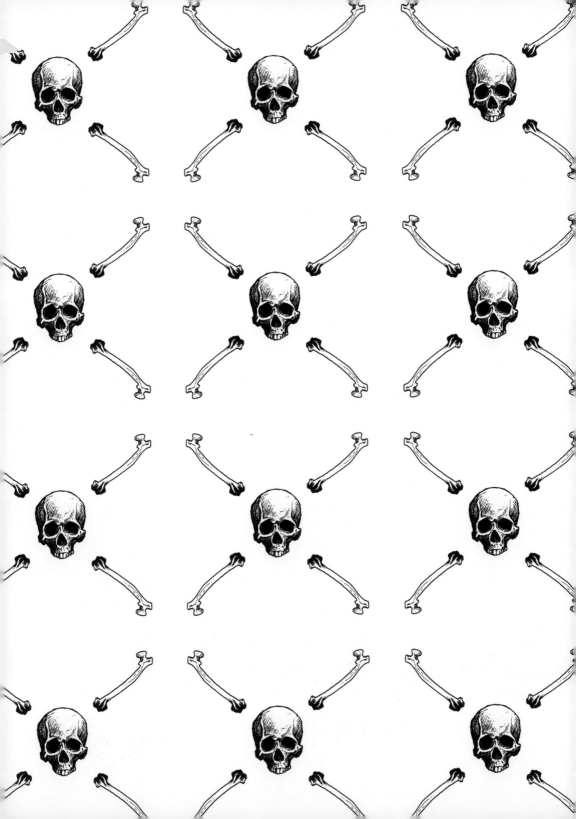

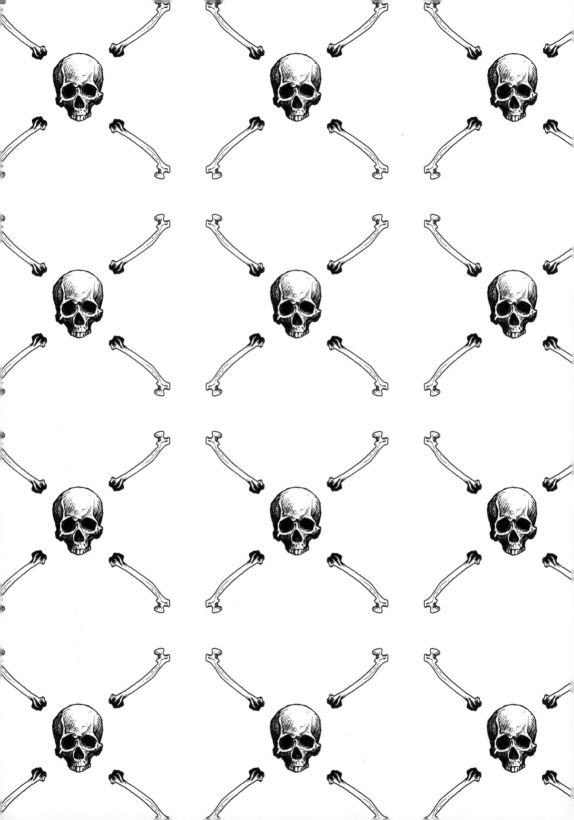

HORROR

BEAST

SCREAM

MORGUE

CREEP

BEST BEFORE
MAY 15

NO MONSTERS
VILLAGERS
UNITED

DON'T
SCREAM

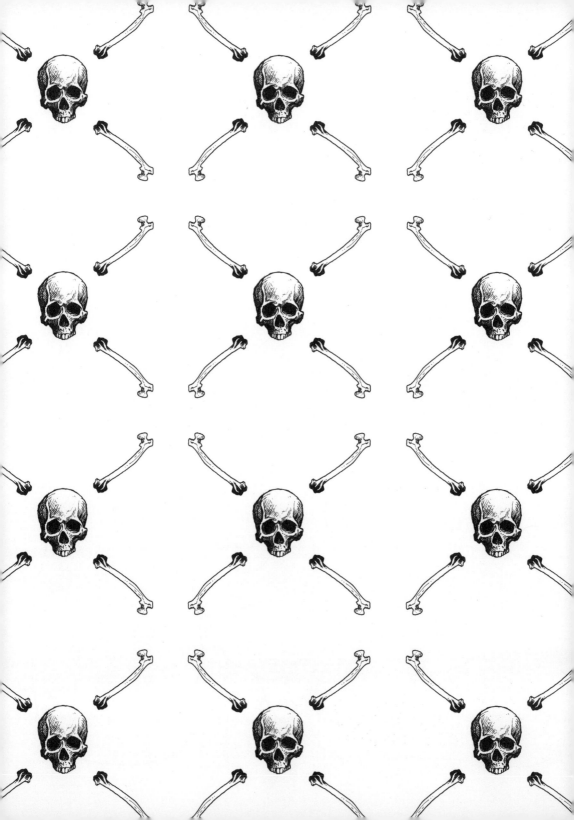

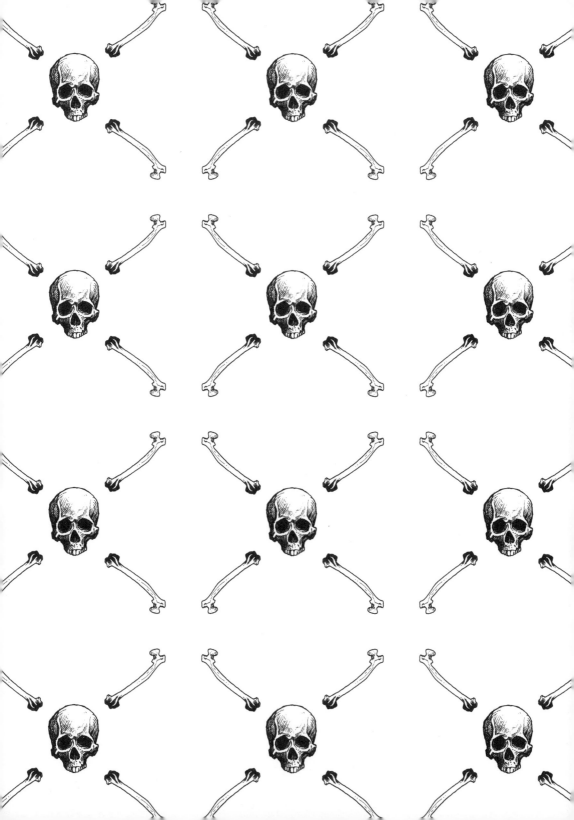

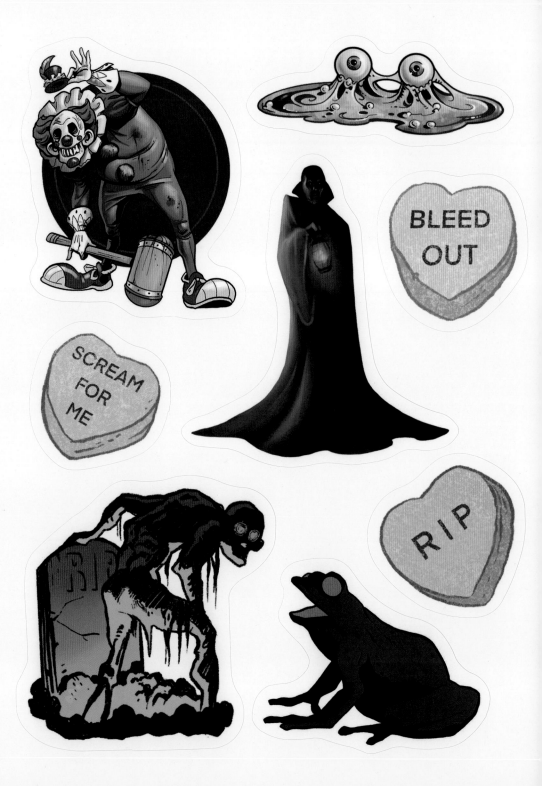

YOU ARE DEAD

DIE SLOWLY

RIP

SCREAM QUEEN

Die Screaming

UNDEAD AND PROUD

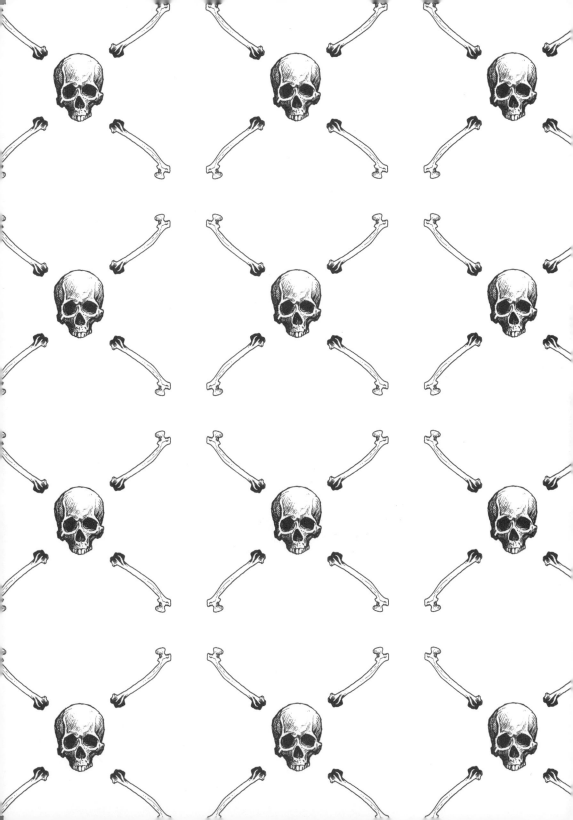

WE BELONG
DEAD

POISON

DON'T
LOSE
YOUR
HEAD

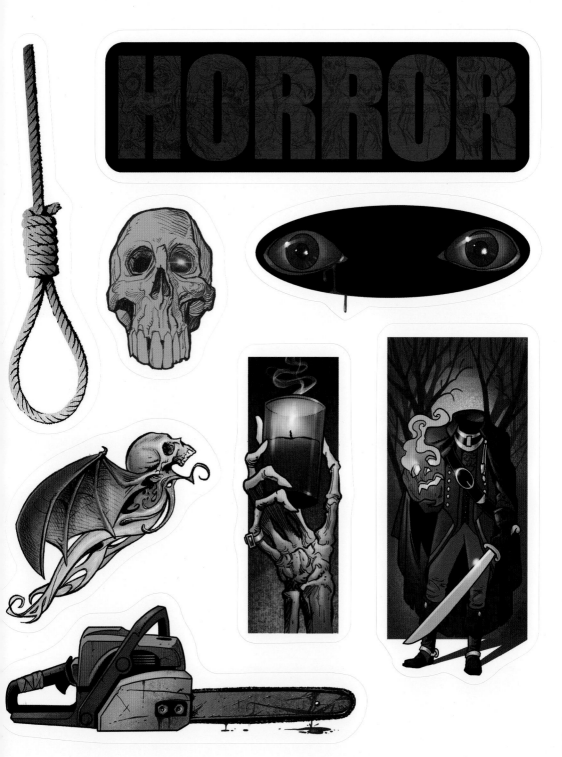

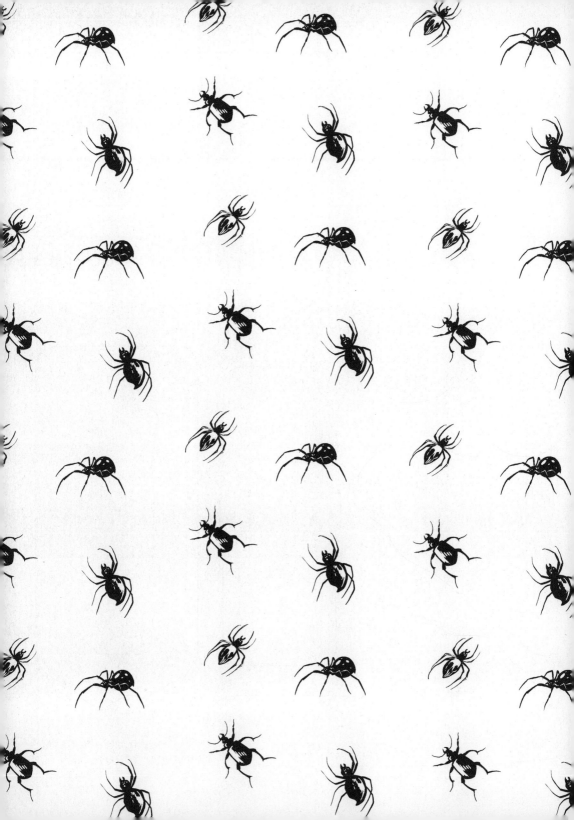

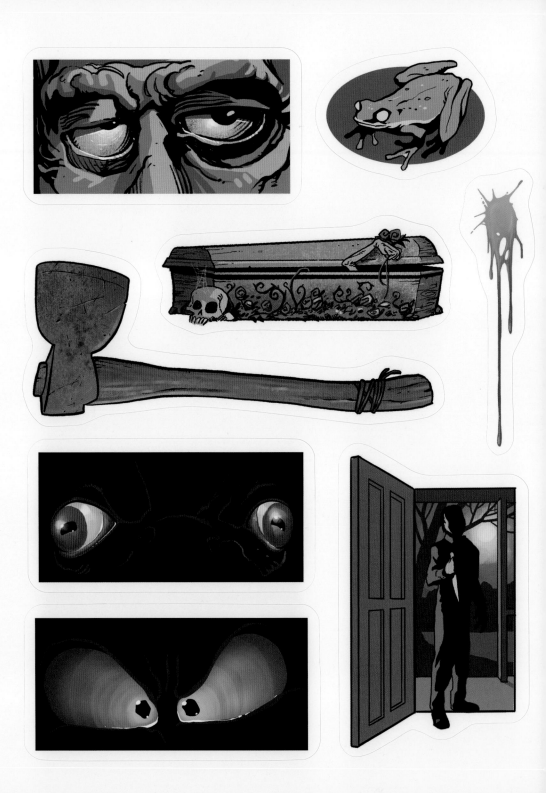

Burke & Hare
Funeral Home
"We put the FUN in Funeral"

Aren't You
DEAD
Yet?

CURIOUS GOODS

Hexes
Spells
Charms
Talismans
Potions
& Poisons

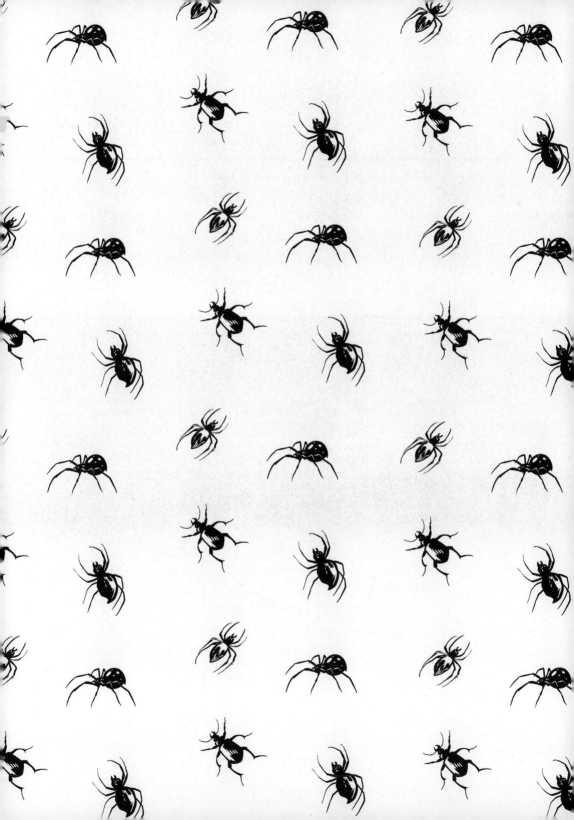

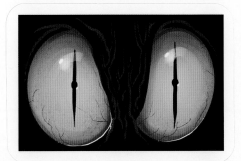

DON'T DIE TONIGHT

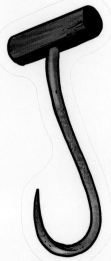

MONSTER

WE'RE SORRY, THE PARTY YOU ARE TRYING TO REACH HAS BEEN

CUT OFF!

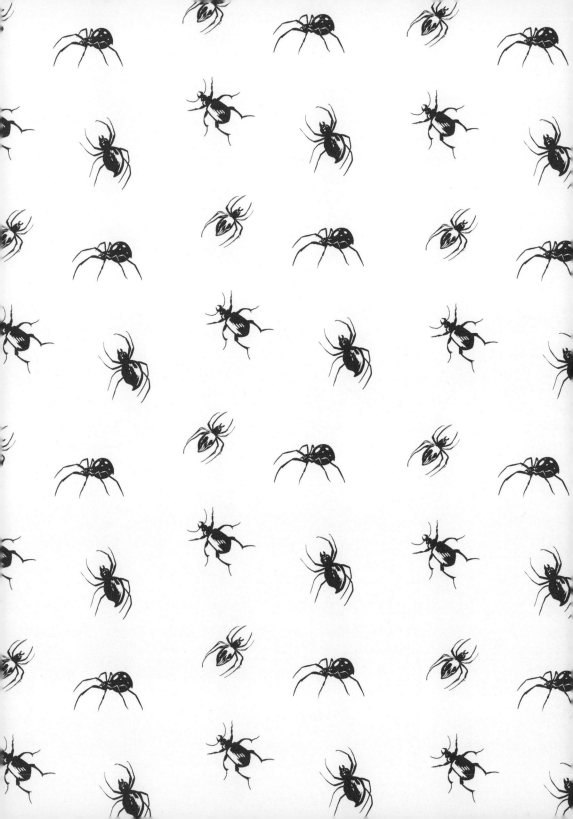

Casketorium

FULL BODY * HEAD ONLY * URNS

Monsieurs Ashe & Duste, props.

BE AFRAID

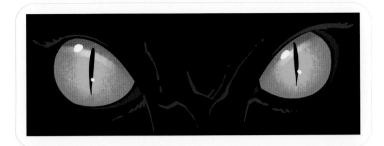

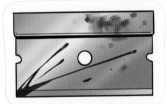

CREATURE OF THE NIGHT

SCREAM

ALL YOU CAN EAT!

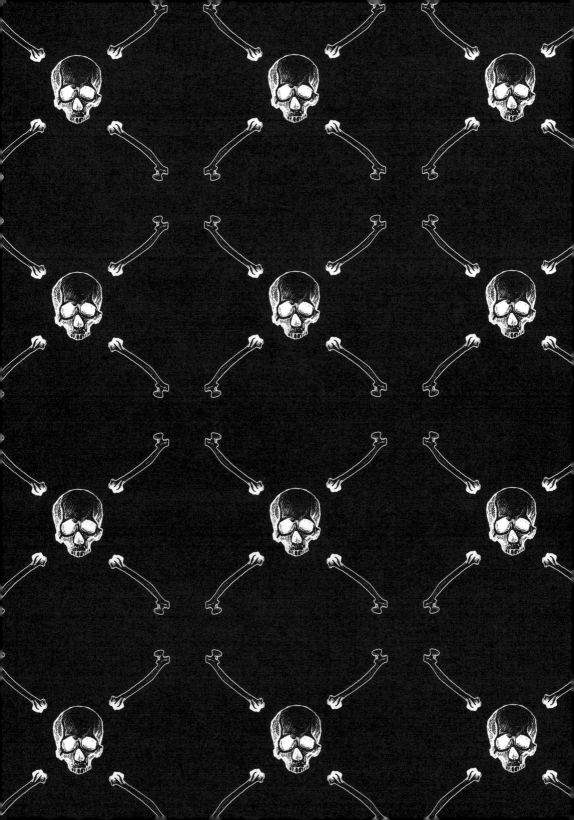

I ♥ HORROR

ROOM FOR RENT

MURDER

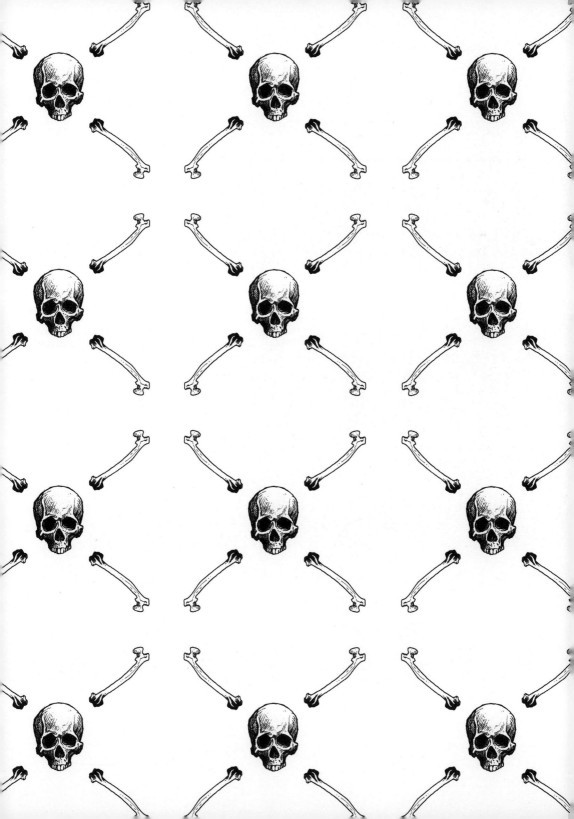

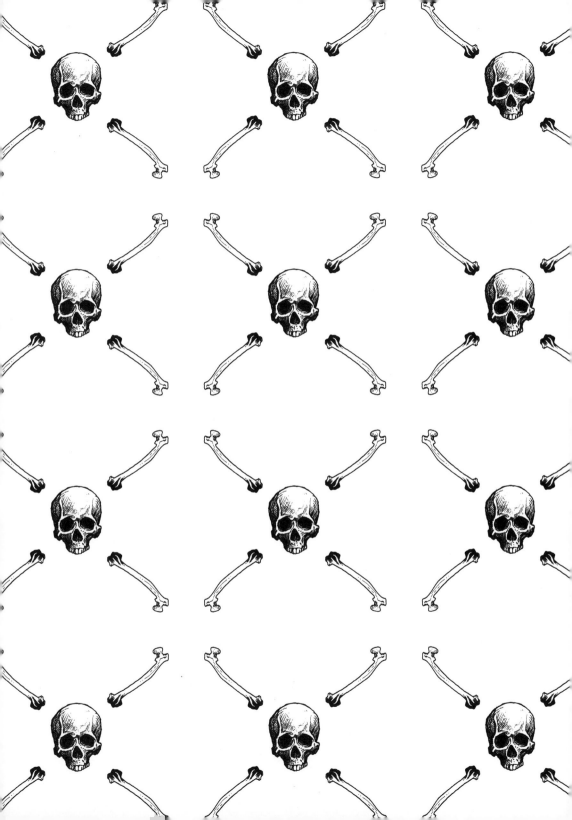

DON'T SCREAM

MONSTER SQUAD

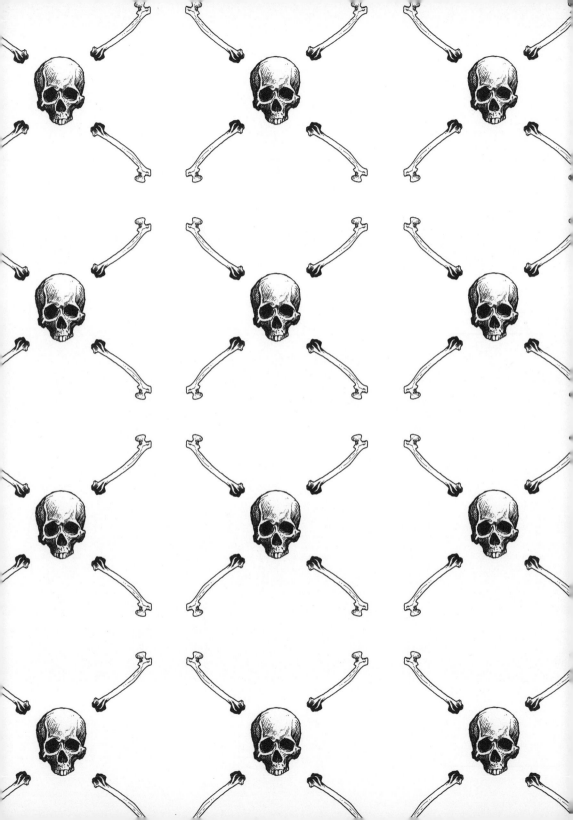

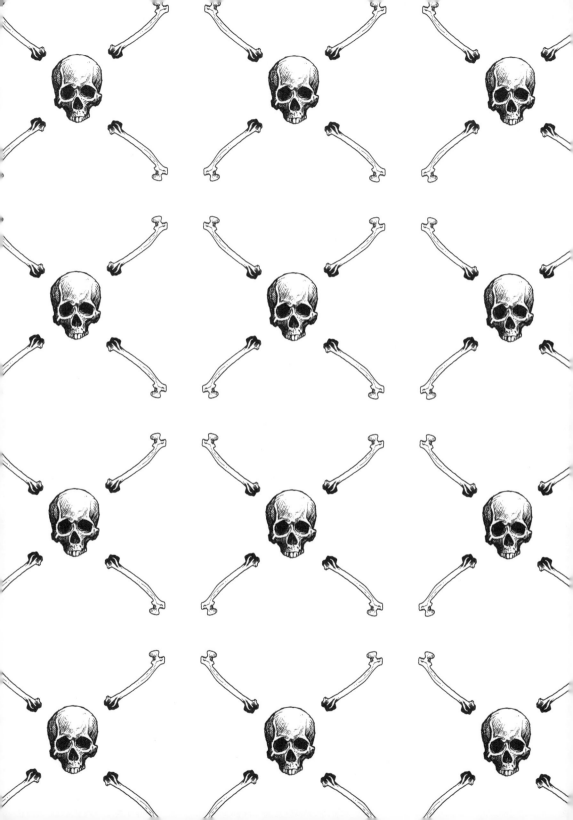

LAST KISS

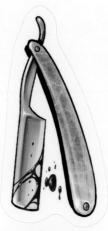

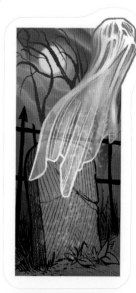

Up the airy mountain,
Down the rushy glen,
We daren't go a-hunting,
For fear of little men.

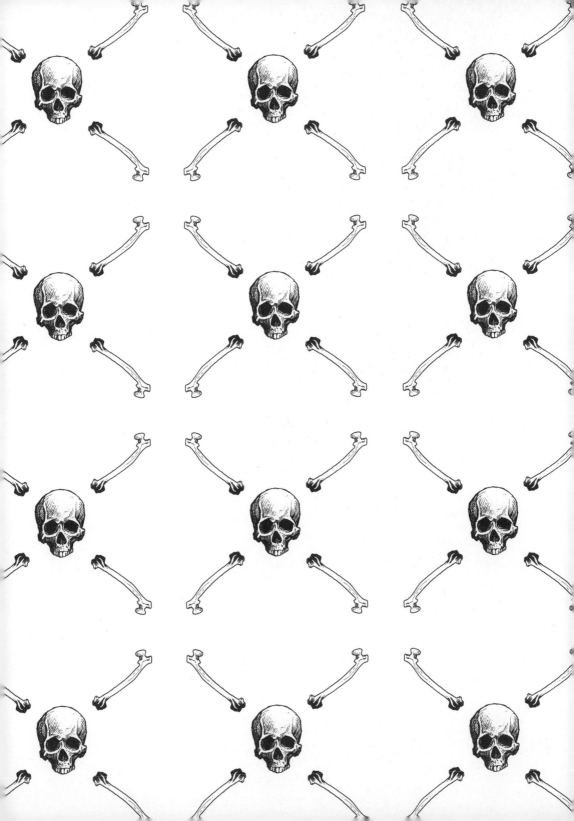

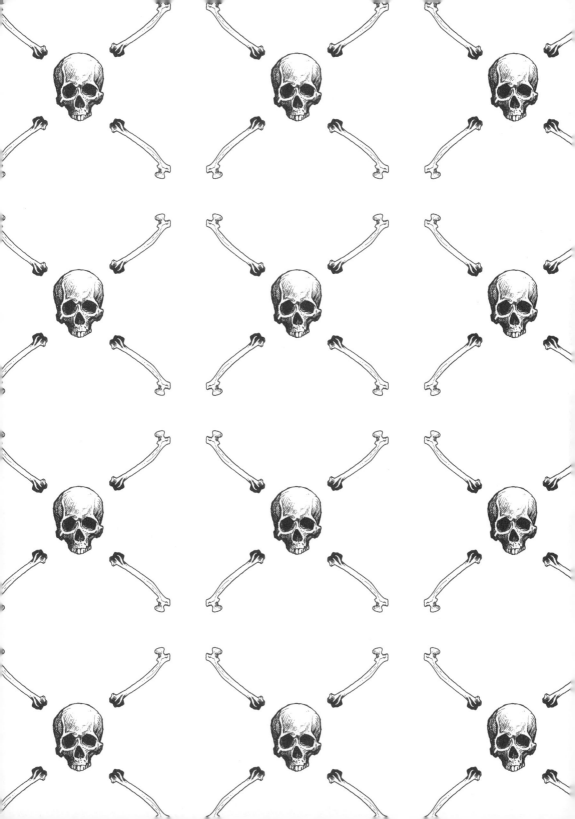

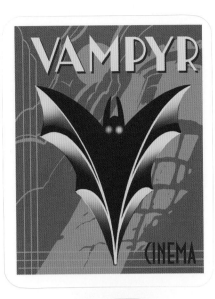

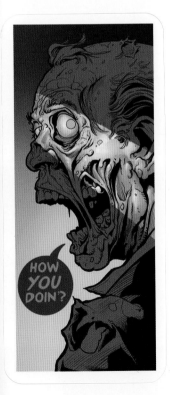

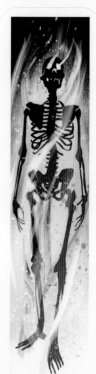